THE SUN

BY LAURA HAMILTON WAXMAN

LERNER PUBLICATIONS COMPANY • MINNEAPOLIS

Lerner Publications Company
A division of Lerner Publishing Group, Inc.
241 First Avenue North
Minneapolis, MN 55401 U.S.A.

Website address: www.lernerbooks.com

Library of Congress Cataloging-in-Publication Data

Waxman, Laura Hamilton.
   The sun / by Laura Hamilton Waxman.
      p.   cm. — (Early bird astronomy)
   Includes index.
   ISBN 978–0–7613–3871–0 (lib. bdg. : alk. paper)
   1. Sun—Juvenile literature. I. Title.
QB521.5.W348 2010
523.7—dc22   2009017995

Manufactured in the United States of America
1 – BP – 12/15/09

CONTENTS

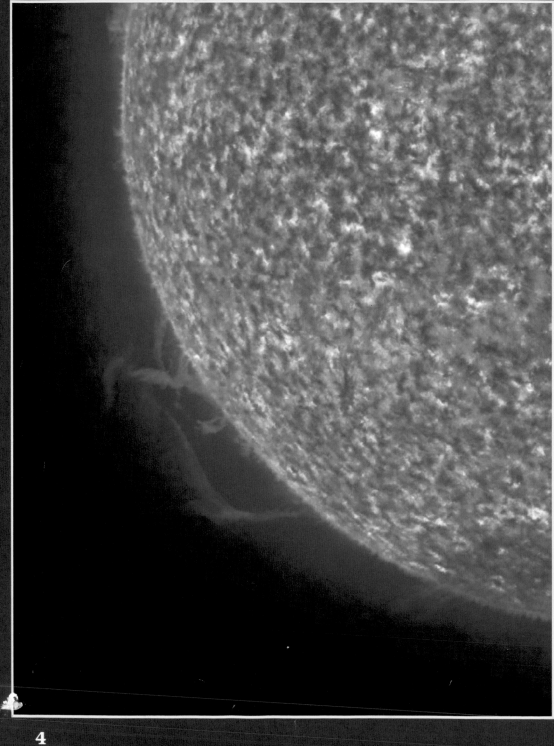

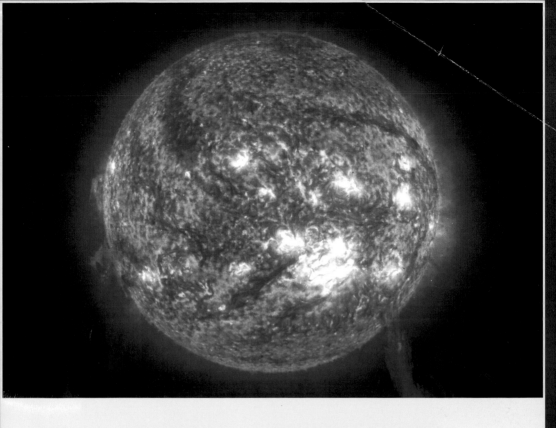

BE A WORD DETECTIVE

Can you find these words as you read about the Sun?
Be a detective and try to figure out what they mean. You
can turn to the glossary on page 46 for help.

astronomers	orbit	solar wind
atmosphere	pinhole camera	spacecraft
auroras	rotates	sunspots
axis	solar flares	telescopes
gravity	solar system	

The Sun keeps our planet warm. Can you feel the Sun's heat on a warm summer day?

CHAPTER 1
EARTH'S STAR

It's a warm summer day. The sky is clear and blue. The Sun shines up above. It looks like a big, glowing ball. It lights up our days. It keeps our planet warm.

The Sun is a star. A star is a huge ball of hot gases. All stars make their own energy. The Sun's energy helps plants on Earth grow. People and animals need the Sun's energy too. Our planet would be cold and dark without the Sun. It would be a planet without life.

Grasses and wildflowers reach their stems toward the Sun. Plants turn the Sun's energy into food.

The Sun is bigger than anything else in our sky. But it is not the biggest star in space. There are billions and billions of stars. Many of them are bigger than the Sun. But the Sun is much closer to Earth than any other star. Close objects look bigger than faraway objects. So the Sun looks much bigger than other stars. It looks much brighter too.

The Sun's glow can be seen just beyond the horizon. As the Sun sets, we can start to see the stars in the night sky.

This special telescope in New Mexico is used to study the Sun.

The Sun is too bright to look at directly. Its light can harm your eyes. People use special telescopes (TEH-luh-skohps) to look at the Sun safely. Telescopes make faraway objects look bigger and closer.

A pinhole camera is another way to look at the Sun. You can make your own pinhole camera. You will need two sheets of stiff paper. You will also need a pin. A grown-up can help you use the pin. Use the pin to poke a hole in the center of one sheet of paper.

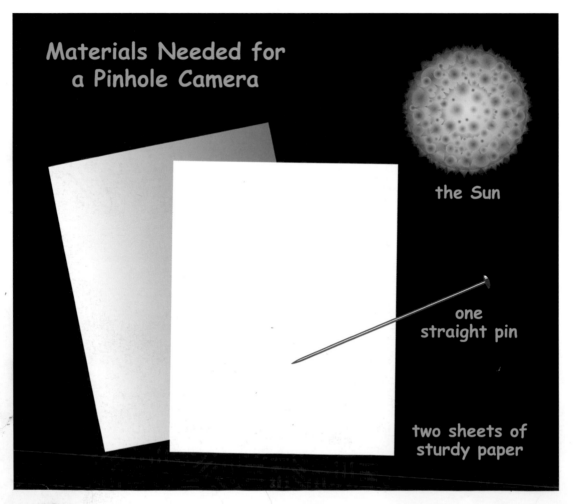

Materials Needed for a Pinhole Camera

the Sun

one straight pin

two sheets of sturdy paper

Take both sheets of paper outside on a sunny day. Hold up your paper with the hole. Let the Sun shine through the hole. Put your second sheet of paper a few inches behind the hole. You will see a bright dot on that piece of paper. The dot is a small picture of the Sun!

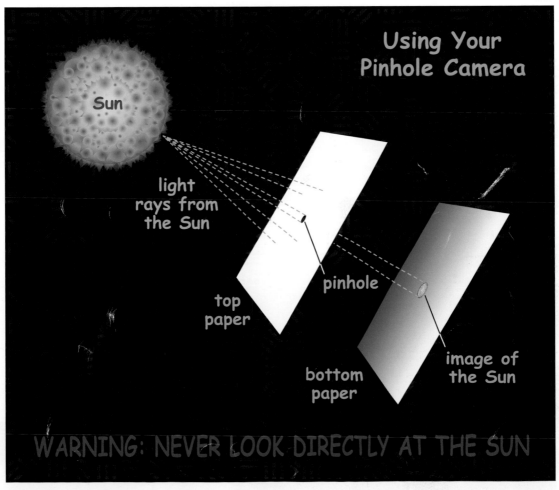

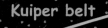
Kuiper belt

Pluto

Neptune

Uranus

Saturn

Jupiter

CHAPTER 2

CENTER OF THE SOLAR SYSTEM

The Earth and the Sun are both part of the solar system. The solar system includes eight planets in all. Smaller rocky objects called asteroids (A-stur-oydz) and comets are also part of the solar system. So are dwarf planets. Dwarf planets are larger than asteroids and comets. But they are smaller than the main planets.

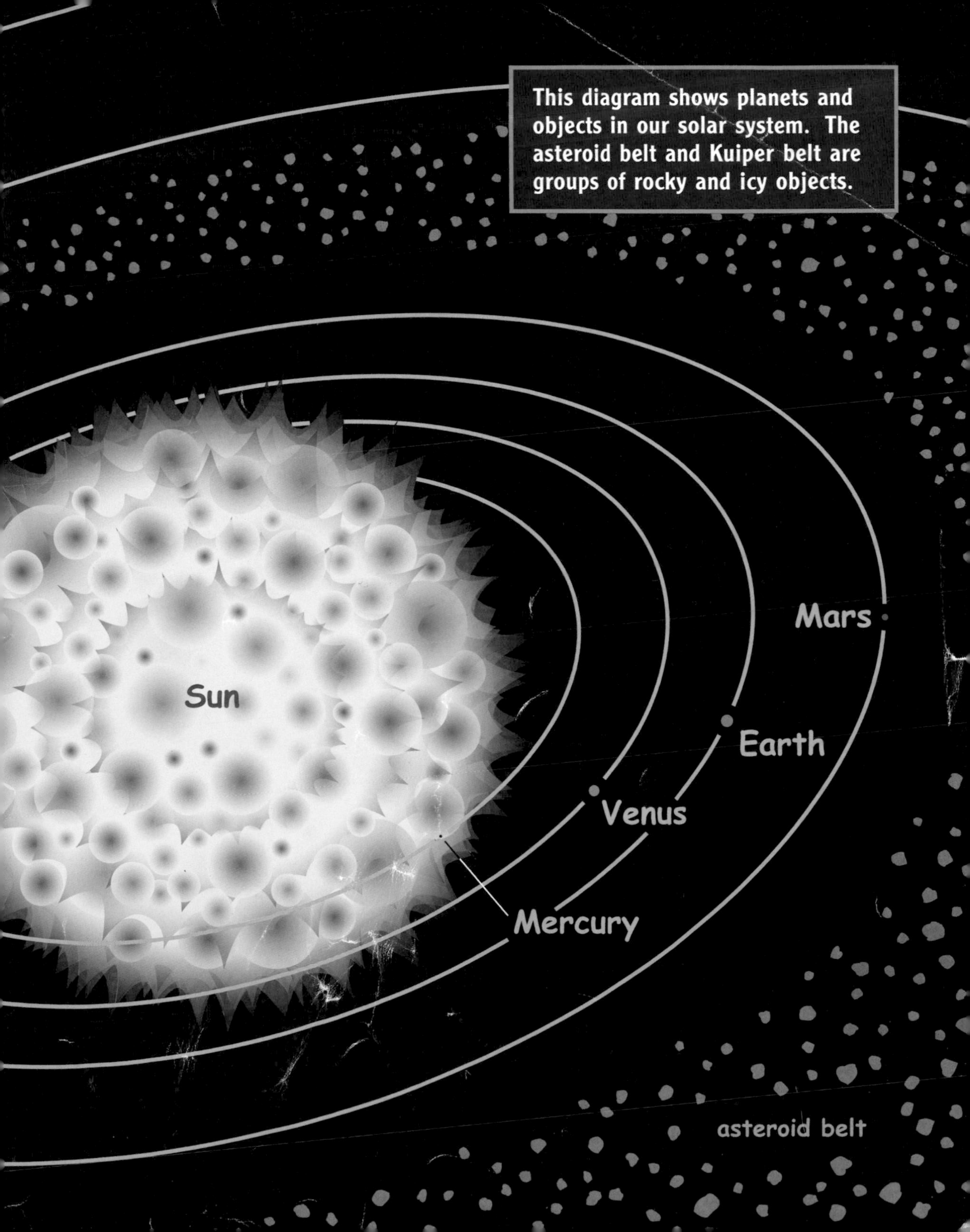

This diagram shows planets and objects in our solar system. The asteroid belt and Kuiper belt are groups of rocky and icy objects.

Mars

Sun

Earth

Venus

Mercury

asteroid belt

The Sun lies at the center of the solar system. Mercury, Venus, Earth, and Mars are the closest planets to the Sun. Jupiter, Saturn, Uranus, and Neptune are the farthest planets.

This picture shows the Sun and all eight planets in order.

This image shows Earth with the Sun in the background.

Earth is the third planet from the Sun. Earth and the Sun are about 93 million miles (150 million kilometers) apart. That's the perfect distance. Earth gets just the right amount of the Sun's heat and light for people to live. Planets closer to the Sun are much too hot. Planets farther away are much too cold.

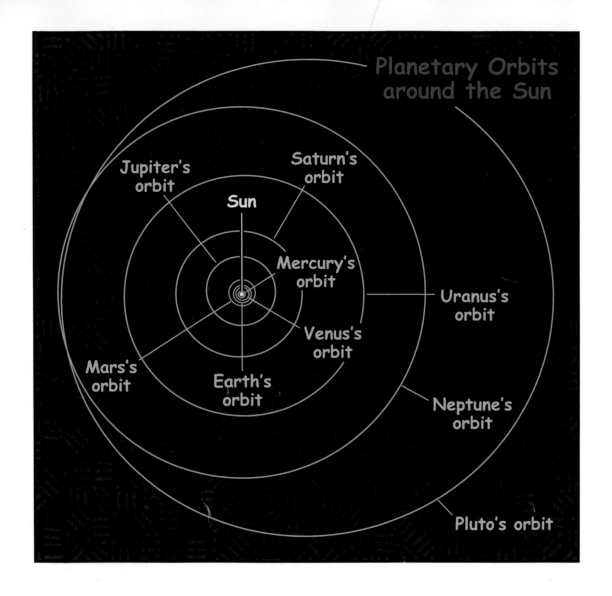

The planets, asteroids, and comets all travel around the Sun. Each one follows its own path. This path is called an orbit. Earth takes a year to travel its orbit once.

The Sun's gravity keeps everything in orbit. Gravity is a force that pulls one object toward another. Bigger objects have more gravity than smaller ones. The Sun is bigger than anything else in the solar system. So its gravity is the strongest. The Sun's gravity keeps Earth and the other planets from floating away.

The planets circle the Sun in our solar system.

This image was taken with special equipment that took a photo every six minutes. Does it look like the Sun is moving as it sets?

CHAPTER 3
DAY AND NIGHT

The Sun looks like it's moving across the sky each day. It seems to rise each morning. It seems to sink down each night. But the Sun is not moving in our sky. Instead, our planet is turning.

Earth always rotates (ROH-tayts). To rotate means to spin like a top. Our planet takes about 24 hours to rotate once. All the other planets rotate too. A planet rotates on its axis (AK-sihs). An axis is an imaginary line that goes through the center of a planet from top to bottom.

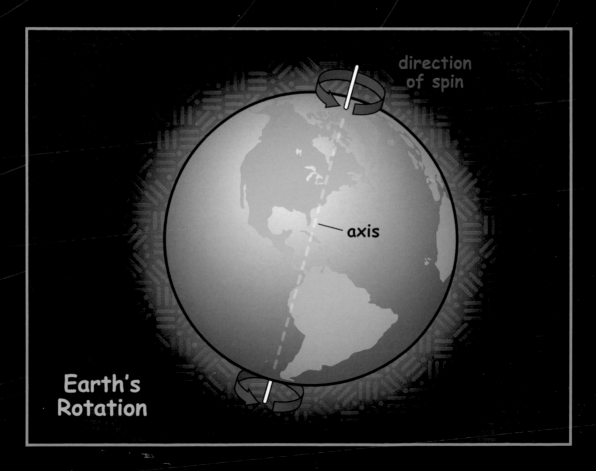

direction of spin

axis

Earth's Rotation

As Earth rotates, different parts of the planet face the Sun. Day comes when your part of Earth rotates toward the Sun. Then the Sun shines on your part of the planet. Night comes when your part of Earth rotates away from the Sun. Then that part of the planet is in darkness.

The surface of Earth that faces the Sun lights up during the day. The surface away from the Sun experiences night.

CHAPTER 4

THE SUN AND THE SEASONS

Do you have cold winters where you live? What about hot summers? The seasons change throughout the year. But Earth stays about the same distance from the Sun. So what causes the change?

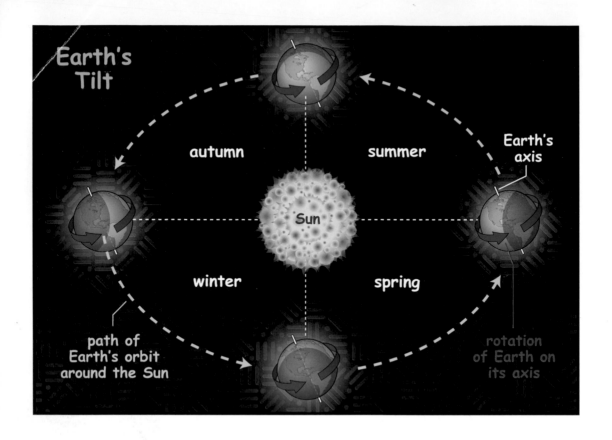

Earth's Tilt

autumn

summer

Earth's axis

Sun

winter

spring

path of Earth's orbit around the Sun

rotation of Earth on its axis

Earth's axis is one reason we have seasons. Earth's axis is tilted. That means Earth is tilted too. Half of Earth tilts toward the Sun. The other half tilts away from the Sun. Earth's top half is called the Northern Hemisphere (HEH-muhs-feer). Earth's bottom half is called the Southern Hemisphere. The United States and Canada are in the Northern Hemisphere.

Earth's orbit is the other reason we have seasons. Our planet moves in its orbit all year long. So Earth's position in space changes throughout the year. In summer, the Northern Hemisphere tilts toward the Sun. It gets a lot of the Sun's heat and light. The air grows warm. Days grow longer. In winter, the Northern Hemisphere tilts away from the Sun.

In autumn, the Northern Hemisphere begins to tilt away from the Sun. When it is autumn in the Northern Hemisphere, it is spring in the Southern Hemisphere.

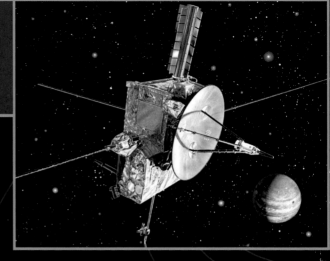

Ulysses is a spacecraft that scientists used to learn about the Sun. What do we call scientists who study the Sun and outer space?

CHAPTER 5
THE SUN UP CLOSE

The Sun is much too hot to visit. But astronomers (uh-STRAH-nuh-murz) have learned about it here on Earth. Astronomers are scientists who study outer space. They use telescopes and other tools to learn about the Sun. Astronomers also use spacecraft to learn about the Sun. Spacecraft are machines that travel to outer space. They have gathered helpful information about the Sun.

The Sun is much bigger than the planets in our solar system. It is about 856,000 miles (1,377,600 km) across. That's wider than one hundred Earths lined up next to one another.

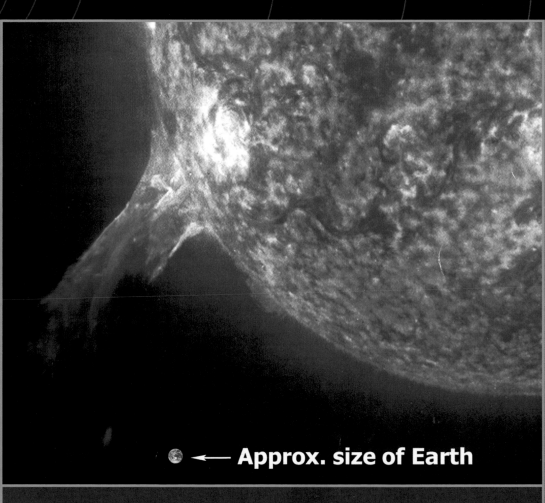

🌍 ⟵ **Approx. size of Earth**

This image gives an idea of how small Earth is when compared to the size of the Sun.

The Sun is also hotter than anything else in the solar system. It is hottest at its center. The center of the Sun is called the core. The core is about 27 million°F (15 million°C). The core is where the Sun makes its energy. We see this energy as light. We feel it as heat.

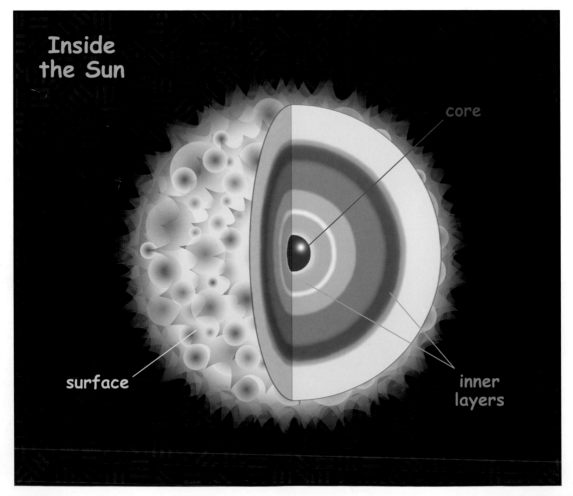

Inside the Sun

core

surface

inner layers

Several layers surround the Sun's core. The layers get cooler toward the Sun's surface. But the surface is still very hot. It is twenty times hotter than a kitchen oven turned all the way up. Beyond the surface is the Sun's atmosphere (AT-muhs-feer). The atmosphere is made of the Sun's outer layers of gases.

The atmosphere of the Sun contains bright, burning gases. Under the surface are even hotter layers.

The Sun's surface is the part of the Sun we can see. It is not hard like Earth's surface. The Sun is made of gases. Gases are light like air. So the Sun doesn't have a solid ground to stand on.

This photo shows bright patches on the Sun. They are places where very hot gases from inside the Sun have reached the surface.

Sometimes dark spots form on the Sun's surface. These spots are called sunspots. They are cooler than other parts of the Sun's surface. Sunspots look small in pictures. But many of them are as big as Earth. Some are much bigger. Sunspots can last for hours, weeks, or months.

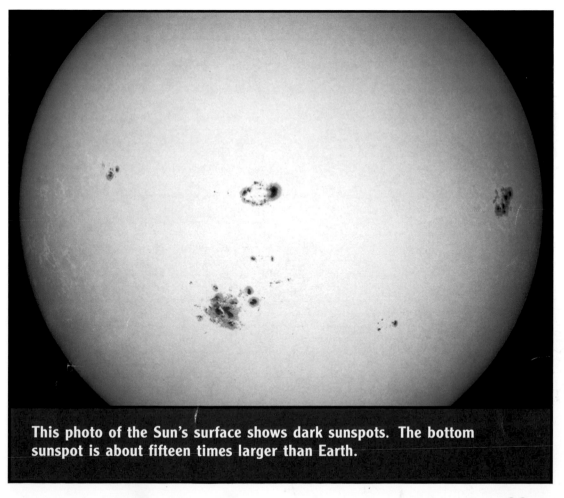

This photo of the Sun's surface shows dark sunspots. The bottom sunspot is about fifteen times larger than Earth.

Sometimes explosions of hot gas happen around sunspots. These explosions send out bursts of energy and light. The bursts are called solar flares.

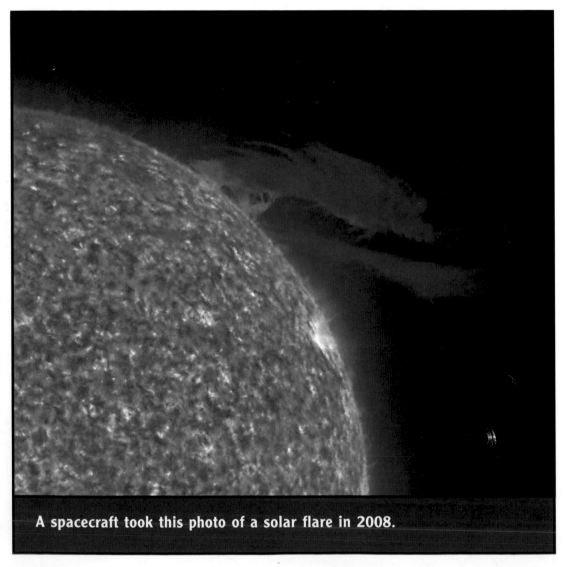

A spacecraft took this photo of a solar flare in 2008.

The Sun sends streams of powerful energy throughout the solar system. This energy is known as solar wind. Solar wind is not like wind on Earth. We cannot feel or hear it. But it is very strong. It can cause problems with electrical power on Earth.

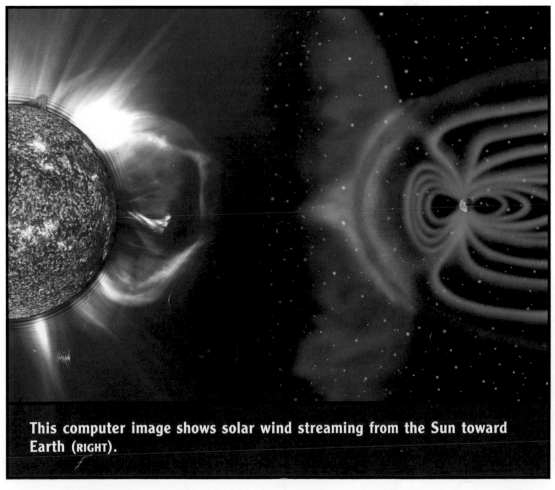

This computer image shows solar wind streaming from the Sun toward Earth (RIGHT).

Solar wind also causes auroras (uh-ROHR-uhz) on Earth. Auroras are colorful lights in the night sky. They shimmer and swirl like waves. Auroras can be seen in the far northern and southern parts of our planet.

This aurora was caused by a solar wind. It lights up the sky over northern Canada.

This painting shows the Egyptian Sun god, Ra (RIGHT). Did people long ago make up stories about Sun gods?

CHAPTER 6
STUDYING THE SUN

People have always been grateful for the Sun's warmth and light. Long ago, they named gods after the Sun. They prayed to those gods. They made up stories about them. People often told stories of sun gods pulling the Sun across the sky.

33

Early astronomers tried to learn about the Sun. Ptolemy was a famous Greek astronomer. He lived nearly two thousand years ago. Ptolemy did not know that the Sun lay at the center of the solar system. He believed the Sun circled around Earth.

Ptolemy is shown in this painting. Like other ancient astronomers, Ptolemy thought the Sun circled Earth.

Another astronomer discovered the truth. His name was Nicolaus Copernicus. Copernicus lived about five hundred years ago. He thought that Earth and the other planets circled the Sun.

In the 1500s, Nicolaus Copernicus figured out that the Sun was at the center of the solar system.

ARISSIMUS · ET · DOCTISSIMUS · DO
R · NICOLAUS · COPERNICUS · TOR
NSIS · CANONICUS · WARMIENS
TRONOMUS · INCOMPARABILIS

Another famous astronomer helped prove that Copernicus was right. His name was Galileo Galilei. Copernicus and Galileo helped people understand the solar system.

This painting shows Galileo Galilei. Galileo used a telescope to help prove that Earth circles the Sun.

But astronomers still had many questions about the Sun. They wondered what our nearest star was really like. They thought spacecraft might help answer their questions.

In the 1900s, astronomers such as George Hale (LEFT) invented better ways to study our Sun.

People began to send spacecraft from Earth in the 1950s. Some of these machines were used to study the Sun. But the spacecraft did not go all the way to the Sun. The Sun's heat would have burned up any spacecraft that came too close.

A series of spacecraft were sent into space during the 1960s to study the Sun. This rocket, carrying *Pioneer 6,* was launched on December 16, 1965.

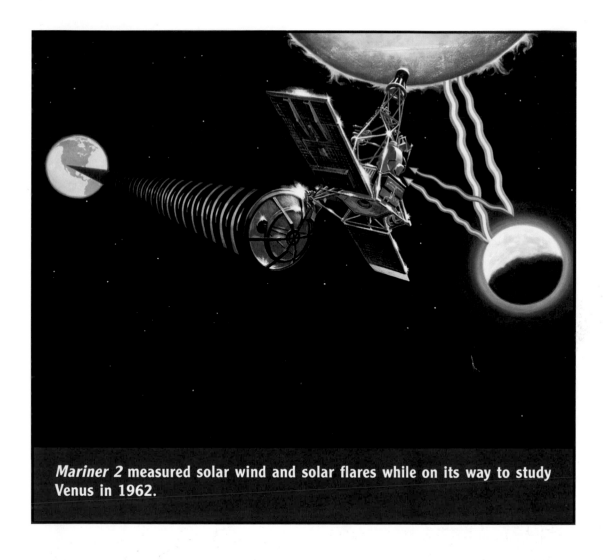

Mariner 2 measured solar wind and solar flares while on its way to study Venus in 1962.

The spacecraft took pictures of the Sun. The spacecraft were also used to measure energy from solar flares and solar wind. This information helped astronomers understand more about how the Sun works.

Spacecraft are still used to study the Sun. *SOHO* and *TRACE* left Earth in the 1990s. *RHESSI, SORCE, STEREO,* and the *Hinode* left Earth in the early 2000s.

Engineers put the finishing touches on the *SOHO* spacecraft.

Every day, these spacecraft send information back to Earth. They are helping us learn more about the Sun. They are helping scientists understand how the Sun's energy affects Earth.

These two spacecraft are known as *STEREO*. They work together to give scientists better images of the Sun.

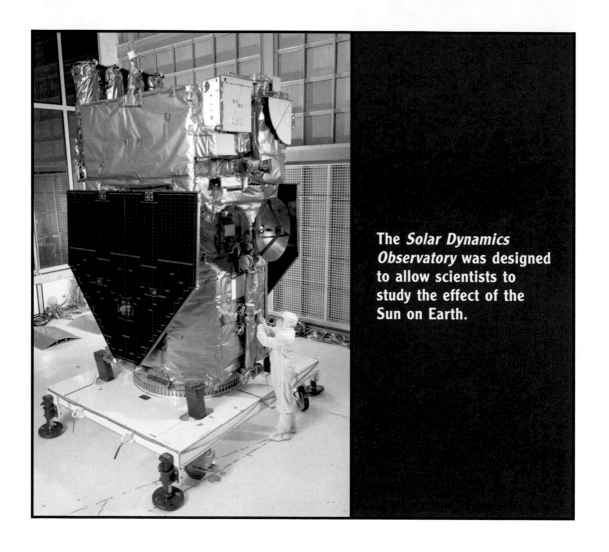

The *Solar Dynamics Observatory* was designed to allow scientists to study the effect of the Sun on Earth.

In 2009, another spacecraft will begin to study the Sun. It is called the *Solar Dynamics Observatory* (*SDO*). The *SDO* will help scientists know when explosions on the Sun are going to happen.

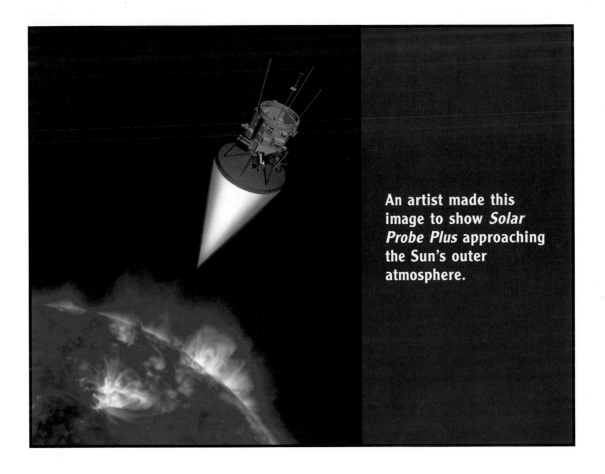

An artist made this image to show *Solar Probe Plus* approaching the Sun's outer atmosphere.

Another spacecraft is planned for takeoff in 2015. *Solar Probe Plus* will be the first spacecraft to go all the way to the Sun's outer atmosphere. The probe is designed to survive the extreme temperatures of the Sun. It will teach scientists more about the solar wind and the Sun's energy. We still have a lot to learn about our nearest star.

ON SHARING A BOOK

When you share a book with a child, you show that reading is important. To get the most out of the experience, read in a comfortable, quiet place. Turn off the television and limit other distractions, such as telephone calls. Be prepared to start slowly. Take turns reading parts of this book. Stop occasionally and discuss what you're reading. Talk about the photographs. If the child begins to lose interest, stop reading. When you pick up the book again, revisit the parts you have already read.

BE A VOCABULARY DETECTIVE

The word list on page 5 contains words that are important in understanding the topic of this book. Be word detectives and search for the words as you read the book together. Talk about what the words mean and how they are used in the sentence. Do any of these words have more than one meaning? You will find the words defined in a glossary on page 46.

WHAT ABOUT QUESTIONS?

Use questions to make sure the child understands the information in this book. Here are some suggestions:

> What did this paragraph tell us? What does this picture show? What do you think we'll learn about next? What is the Sun made of? How does the Sun affect life on Earth? How do scientists study the Sun?

If the child has questions, don't hesitate to respond with questions of your own, such as What do *you* think? Why? What is it that you don't know? If the child can't remember certain facts, turn to the index.

INTRODUCING THE INDEX

The index helps readers get information without searching throughout the whole book. Turn to the index on page 48. Choose an entry, such as *auroras,* and ask the child to use the index to find out what auroras are. Repeat with as many entries as you like. Ask the child to point out the differences between an index and a glossary. (The index helps readers find information quickly, while the glossary tells readers what words mean.)

LEARN MORE ABOUT
THE SUN

BOOKS

Hoffman, Sara. *The Little Book of Space.* Minnetonka, MN: Two-Can, 2005. In this book, the author describes the bodies in the solar system as well as different missions to space.

Jackson, Ellen. *The Worlds around Us.* Minneapolis: Millbrook Press, 2007. This illustrated book is for anyone who wonders what it would be like to take a trip through the solar system.

Tocci, Salvadore. *Experiments with the Sun and Moon.* New York: Children's Press, 2003. This author invites readers to try hands-on activities that are fun and educational.

Vogt, Gregory L. *Stars.* Minneapolis: Lerner Publications Company, 2010. This book has more information about stars such as the Sun.

WEBSITES

Extreme Space
http://solarsystem.nasa.gov/kids/index.cfm
The National Aeronautics and Space Administration (NASA) created this astronomy website just for kids.

The Space Place
http://spaceplace.nasa.gov/en/kids/
Go to this Web page of NASA's for activities, quizzes, and games all about outer space.

The Sun
http://kids.nineplanets.org/portfoli.htm
This astronomy website offers lots of kid-friendly information about the Sun.

Sun: Our Star
http://solarsystem.nasa.gov/planets/profile.cfm?Object
=Sun&Display=Kids
This NASA website about the Sun is geared just for kids.

GLOSSARY

astronomers (uh-STRAH-nuh-murz): scientists who study outer space

atmosphere (AT-muhs-feer): the layer of gases that surrounds a star or a planet

auroras (uh-ROHR-uhz): colorful lights that swirl in the night sky in the northern and southern parts of Earth

axis (AK-sihs): an imaginary line that goes through a planet or moon from top to bottom. A planet or moon spins on its axis.

gravity: a force that pulls one object toward another

orbit: the circular path a planet, moon, or other space object travels in space. *Orbit* can also mean to move along this path.

pinhole camera: a simple device that can be used to look at the Sun

rotates (ROH-tayts): spins around like a top

solar flares: explosions of hot gas on the Sun

solar system: the Sun and a group of planets and other objects that travel around it

solar wind: energy that shoots out from the Sun after an explosion

spacecraft: machines that travel from Earth to outer space

sunspots: cooler places on the Sun's surface that look like black dots

telescopes (TEH-luh-skohps): instruments that make faraway objects appear bigger and closer

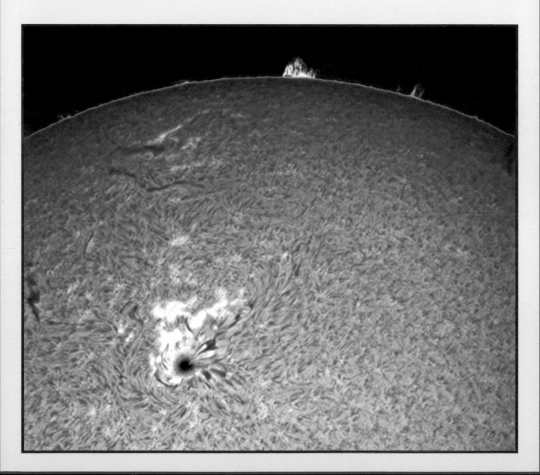

INDEX

Pages listed in **bold** type refer to photographs.

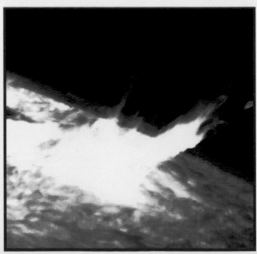